A SUNNY DAY

Kate Petty

Illustrated by Jacqueline Wood

AWARD PUBLICATIONS

Joe wants the sun to shine all day today. Mum has promised a picnic on the beach. What do they need to take with them?

Mum wants to set off early,
before it gets too hot.

Don't forget the beach
umbrella!

3

Dad has plenty to do in the garden. All growing things need the sun. The flowers open and bend towards it.

Out in the fields the wheat is being harvested. The sun has helped it to grow and ripen.

The sun goes behind a cloud
just as Mum and Joe arrive at
the beach. Everything looks
dull – but not for long.
The sun comes out again!

When the sun is bright, the shadows are dark. Shadows are made when things block the path of the sun's light. It is cooler in the shadow of the beach umbrella.

Joe plays with his shadow.

Sometimes it is behind him.
Sometimes it is on one side.

Joe's shadow seems to be getting shorter. It must be nearly midday, when the sun is right overhead.

Shadows show the time on a sundial. You can make one for yourself.

You need:
a square of thick card
a lump of Plasticine
paints, crayons or felt tips
for colouring
a sunny day!

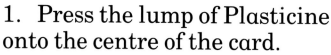

1.

2.

1. Press the lump of Plasticine onto the centre of the card.
2. Push the pencil firmly into the Plasticine at an angle, as shown. This is your pointer.
3. Take your dial outside to a place which is sunny all day long.

3.

4. Every hour – or every half-hour if you can – rule a line along the shadow made by the pointer. Write the number of the hour at the end of each line.

4.

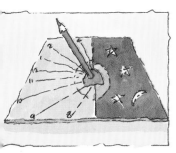

5. Decorate your sundial. Leave your sundial where it is. On the next sunny day you will be able to tell the time from the shadow of the pointer.

11

On the beach it is very hot. Mum wants Joe to wear his sunhat. She rubs sun cream on his skin so that the sun doesn't burn him.

Even the sand feels hot.
Joe can play in the sea
when he wants to cool off.

This is another good
way to stay cool!

Joe loves hot, sunny days in summer. He likes sunny days at other times of the year, too.

In spring, the sun warms the earth. Green shoots start to appear.

Gentle autumn sunshine
ripens the fruit. Butterflies
enjoy its warmth.

The sun in winter makes the
frost and snow glisten and
sparkle.

15

Our world is forever circling the sun. It takes a year to go round the sun once.

Places near the Equator, like the Sahara Desert in Africa, have strong sunshine all year round.

Northern Greenland, near the North Pole, has no sunshine at all in midwinter.

The world spins like a top as it circles the sun. It takes 24 hours to spin round once.

It is day-time in those parts of the world which are lit up by the sun. It is night-time in the parts which face away from the sun.

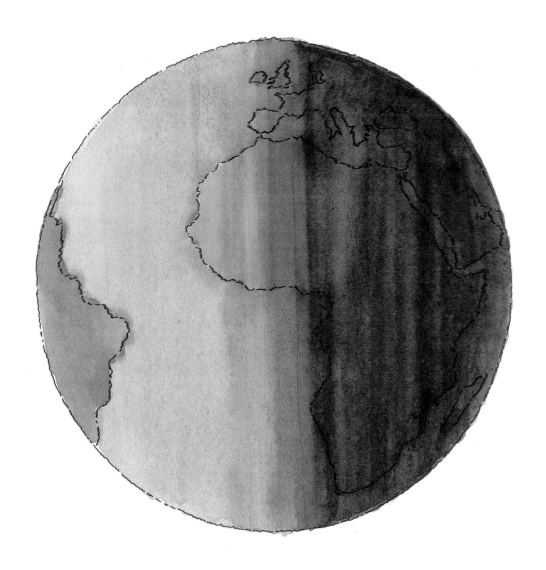

It is still light when Mum
and Joe come home. Dad is
watering the flowers. After the
hot day they need a drink too.

The sun casts long shadows as it sinks lower in the sky. It's still very warm outside. Joe has his supper in the garden.

Now it is evening and Joe is
ready for bed. The sun is setting.
It looks red, and the sky is many
different beautiful colours.
Joe watches the sun go down.

It's strange to think that on
the other side of the world
there are children just waking
up to a sunny day!

sunny day words

beach

beach umbrella

shadow

sundial

sunhat

sunset